THE PURIM STORY

By Sarah Mazor

Illustrator: Marscheila Christyani

-

THE STORY OF PURIM!

The holiday of Purim is celebrated every year in the month of Adar, four weeks before Passover. Purim is plural for the word *Pur,* which means "lot". It refers to the evil plot of Haman who casted lots to determine the best day to eliminate the Jewish people who lived in the Persian Empire during the days of King Achashverosh (Xerxes I).

Purim celebrates the wonderful miracle and the reversal of fortune experienced by the Jews of Persia (Iran). The customs of Purim include hearing the Scroll of Esther (the Megillah) read in the synagogue; gifting foods and delicacies to family, friends and neighbors; giving charity to the poor; and eating a festive meal. Another inextricable part of Purim and perhaps the most enjoyable one is the tradition that is primarily but not exclusively carried out by kids: Dressing in a myriad of colorful costumes. Masquerading on Purim commemorates the fact that the miracle of Purim was not obvious but disguised as natural events (i.e. Queen Esther's marriage and her influence on her husband, the powerful King of Persia).

[Author's Note: The Scroll of Esther identifies Mordechai as Esther's cousin rather than her uncle. However, as Morderchai adopted and raised young Esther upon the demise of her parents, *The Purim Story* assumes that Queen Esther respectfully addressed her cousin as "Uncle Morderchai."]

Thank you for purchasing

The PURIM Story

We hope you enjoy this book

Books make the best presents, for they are the gifts that keep on giving!

Inside This Book:

- Glossary
- The Story of Purim
- Customs and Traditions
  - *Megillah Reading*
  - *Festive Meal*
  - *Mishloach Manot*
  - *Charity to the Poor*
  - *Costumes and Masquerading*

GLOSSARY

ACHASHVEROSH THE KING OF PERSIA: King Xerxes I, who ruled the Persian Empire during the 4th century BCE.

CHAG PURIM: Holiday of Purim

ESTHER: Girl's name, origin Persian. The name Esther was first given to Jewish girls in honor of the courageous Queen Esther, who saved the Jews of Persia from annihilation.

HAMANTASHEN: Yiddish for Haman's pockets. Triangular-shaped pastries. Hamentashen are eaten on Purim to commemorate the Jews' escape from Haman's wicked plans. One explanation for the triangular shape of the pastries is that Haman wore three cornered hats.

HASHEM: Literally means *The Name*, which is how Jews refer to God.

L'CHAIM: Traditional toast *To Life*

MEGILLAH: Scroll (usually made of parchment).

MEGILLAT ESTHER: Scroll of Esther, the Biblical Book of Esther.

MISHLOACH MANOT: Literally, sending of portions. This refers to the custom of gifting baskets of food and drink on Purim, to family, friends and neighbors. (Also known as *Mishloach Manos* and *Shalach Manos*.)

Have you heard the amazing story
Of Uncle Mordechai's fame and glory,
The favorite uncle of Queen Esther,
Whom wicked Haman loved to pester?

It all began with a king's quest
For a queen; he desired the best.
He chose the prettiest girl in town
To wear the majestic royal crown.

The new queen was given a wedding ring
By Achashverosh, the Persian king,
Who did not know then that this dame
Also had a Hebrew name.

Esther was Hadassah too,
A name so common for a Jew.
But this was a fact, Esther the bride
Had no choice, she just had to hide.

For she was given a major task,
A big huge favor she had to ask,
A most important crucial thing,
Of Achashverosh the Persian king.

It was Uncle Mordechai
Who told the queen that she may die
Unless she found a speedy way
To stop Haman and save the day.

Wicked Haman, the minister,
Plotted something sinister.
He convinced the king to sign a bill,
All the Persian Jews to kill.

The queen was oh so very smart
And knew exactly where to start.
The king and Haman she invited
To a garden party. They were delighted.

And there to wicked Haman's dismay
Things went terribly astray
As Queen Esther then disclosed
What wicked Haman had proposed.

"Did you know, my king," she said.
"Wicked Haman wants me dead.
And my uncle Mordechai
And all the Jews of Persia. Why?"

The king was very, very mad.
"Oh wicked Haman, you are bad!"
He tore to pieces the decree
And then hung Haman on a tree.

And Uncle Mordechai became
A man of fortune and of fame.
Appointed as the king's right hand,
He brought peace and riches to the land.

To commemorate the day
We have the Purim holiday.
With gratitude and lots of cheer,
We celebrate it every year.

Thousands of years have now gone by
Since Queen Esther and Uncle Mordechai
Secured the Persian king's consent
To halt wicked Haman's bad intent.

And so since then on this very date
Jews thank Hashem and celebrate.
And one and all take on the mission
To keep up with the fun tradition.

Megillah Reading

The Scroll of Esther gives an account
Of what the queen had to surmount
To save herself and to save her nation
From Haman's proposed annihilation.

FESTIVE MEAL

On Chag Purim it is the fashion
To eat delicious *hamentashen*
And feast on gourmet food so fine
And raise *L'chaim* with kosher wine.

MISHLOACH MANOT – GIFTING OF FOOD

Another one of the holiday duties
Is spreading goodwill with baskets of goodies.
Gifting candy and cookies or even a stew
To neighbors and friends and family too.

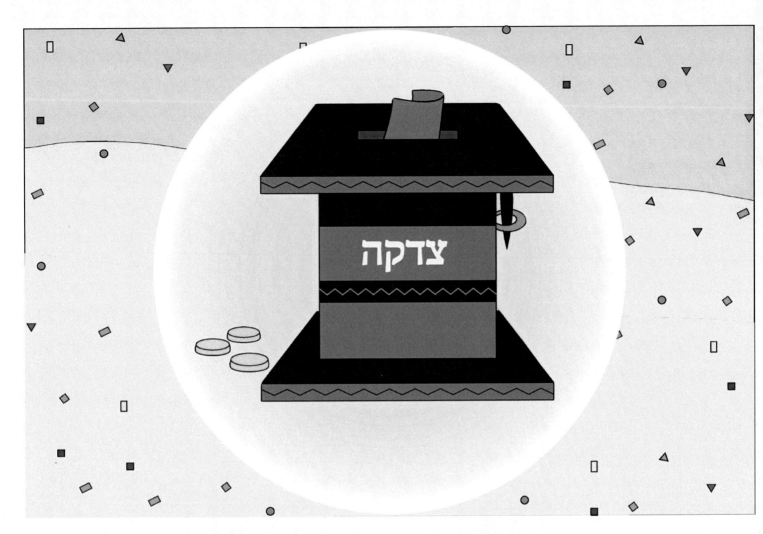

CHARITY TO THE POOR

Giving and sharing is another way
To celebrate this joyous day.
Helping others who are in need
Is truly always a very good deed.

COSTUMES AND MASQUERADES

Masquerading is so much fun
As a king or a granny wearing a bun.
Or a lion or a tiger or a giraffe
Or anything that makes people laugh.

Check Out the Rest of the MazorBooks Library

Children's Books with Good Values

www.MazorBooks.com

www.mazorbooks.wordpress.com
www.facebook.com/mazorbooks
www.twitter.com/mazorbooks

Made in the USA
Middletown, DE
16 March 2016